Moses

Scripture text from
The Contemporary English Version

• *Slaves in Egypt*	2	• *The Ten Commandments*	20
• *The Call of Moses*	8	• *Toward the Promised Land*	26
• Set Free	14	• *Human Rights*	32

Master Books

CHAPTER 1
Slaves in Egypt

Sir John Edward Poynter
(1836-1919)
Great Britain
Israel's Slavery in Egypt
Oil on canvas

This painting is full of detail. Look at the bright colors of the temple decorations. Look at the many people needed to pull the huge statue. How many do you think there are?

© Bridgeman-Giraudon / Guildhall Art Gallery, London

About 1250 B.C.

History

Carving in the Temple of Karnak, north of Luxor in Egypt

The children of Israel had been in Egypt for many years. They lived off their flocks of sheep and goats, and grew what they could. They were happy and thriving as a people.

Suddenly, what seemed like overnight, their world was turned upside down. A new king of Egypt (Pharaoh) let everyone know that he didn't trust the foreigners who lived so near his borders. So he put these foreigners to hard labor* and split up the families. He even gave orders that all male children should be killed.

The Israelites ended up being harassed, threatened and enslaved to Pharaoh. These hard times went on for years. No one could foresee an end to it all. The people wondered whether the God of their ancestors Abraham, Isaac and Jacob was capable of doing anything about it. Many became more and more hopeless.

* Hard labor
Egyptian carvings show details of Pharaoh's work camps – slaves looking for water, mixing clay, carrying loads, making bricks, drying them in the sun and carrying them to the building site. While all this was going on, guards armed with spears patrolled the site.

** Many centuries later
In 1947, near the Dead Sea, a shepherd boy found ancient copies of all the Old Testament books, including those accounts Moses wrote about the Israelites' flight from Egypt. The five books of Moses are called the Pentateuch and are eyewitness accounts of historical events.

Memories of Slavery

The story of those days of slavery was recorded by Moses before the Israelites entered the Promised Land. The message of the Exodus is so powerful that the Jews of today also remember the freedom from captivity in Egypt. The Passover holiday is celebrated today to commemorate God's miraculous deliverance of the Israelites in the time of Moses, and to remind both Jews and Gentiles that God always keeps his word. This is a source of comfort for those who believe in Jehovah.

Making bricks in Nepal

Bible

Hard Slavery

Exodus 1.8-14; 2.23-25

Many years later a new king came to power. He did not know what Joseph had done for Egypt, and he told the Egyptians:

There are too many of those Israelites in our country, and they are becoming more powerful than we are. If we don't outsmart them, their families will keep growing larger. And if our country goes to war, they could easily fight on the side of our enemies and escape from Egypt.

The Egyptians put slave bosses in charge of the people of Israel and tried to wear them down with hard work. Those bosses forced them to build the cities of Pithom and Rameses, where the king could store his supplies. But even though the Israelites were mistreated, their families grew larger, and they took over more land. Because of this, the Egyptians hated them worse than before and made them work so hard that their lives were miserable. The Egyptians were cruel to the people of Israel and forced them to make bricks and to mix mortar and to work in the fields.

After the death of the king of Egypt, the Israelites still complained because they were forced to be slaves. They cried out for help, and God heard their loud cries. He did not forget the promise he had made to Abraham, Isaac, and Jacob, and because he knew what was happening to his people, he felt sorry for them.

Joseph

Joseph was one of the twelve sons of Jacob (also called Israel). He was sold by his jealous brothers to traders on their way to Egypt. Years later, Joseph became the second most important official in Egypt, second only to the Pharaoh himself! With his wisdom, Joseph was able to help the Egyptians survive a great famine. You can find this story in the book of Genesis, chapters 37 to 50.

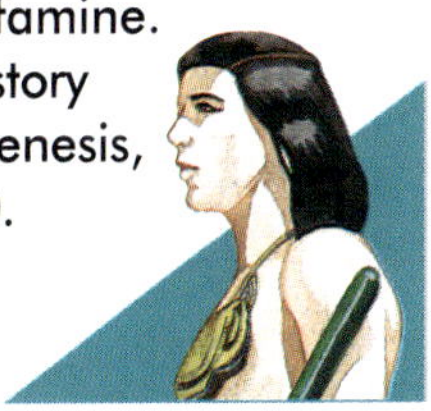

Children of Israel

This is the name for the people of the Bible. They regarded Israel (also called Jacob), the son of Isaac and grandson of Abraham, as their ancestor. The children of Israel are also known by the names Israelites, Hebrews or Jews.

Remembered

God had promised to give Abraham descendants "more numerous than the stars in the sky," and a land "rich with milk and honey" that would one day belong to his descendants.

Today

Oppression

Foreigners

Sometimes people are forced to leave their place of birth. They go elsewhere in order to escape from poverty or trouble, to look for work, to try to find a place where they are treated better and can be happy. Wherever they go they are treated as strangers or foreigners: "You're not from around here. What are you up to?"

Refused a Welcome

In many parts of the world, foreigners are looked down on, and sometimes they are taken advantage of or harassed. Some people even dare to say that foreigners have no rights. They would like to send the foreigners among them back to their own country. Such people fail to understand that being human means welcoming and sharing!

Oppression

In today's world, oppression takes many forms. Oppression happens when people are deprived of land that they have a right to, when refugees are dumped in camps or compounds, when people are sent to prison for what they believe, when people are not given a fair wage, or when their dignity is taken away.

Slavery

Slavery means depriving a person or a group of people of their freedom to think, to act, to work, to travel, or to believe. Slavery exists even today! It happens when human beings are forced to work illegally for very little money, when children are misused by business, or when unjust laws lead to torture or death.

Crying Out to God

People who are oppressed begin to give up and lose hope. Their burden becomes heavier and heavier. They no longer have the strength to fight back. They think that their oppressors are too powerful. Then they turn to God with a shout for help. They cry out in distress, "Only you, Lord, can break our chains!"

Intolerable

In our world today,
there is money to spare,
so it's hard to believe
there are places where
people work till they drop
in inhuman conditions.
To speak up means to lose your job,
dismissed with no pay,
or perhaps beaten up
for trying to say, "It's unjust!"

In our world today,
golden words on high
speak of justice and freedom,
but many still die,
murdered and tortured.
To be killed for the color of your skin,
with no say in your future
is to know, "It's unjust!"

Can we leave them alone
crying to God for help?
Who'll remove the gag
and let them shout:
"Justice, at last!"

CHAPTER 2

The Call of Moses

Marc Chagall (1887-1985) and
Charles Marcq (born 1923)
Moses before the burning bush
Jacques Simon Gallery, Reims
Stained glass from Metz Cathedral

Moses looks amazed. The fiery colors fall from the heavens. What colors would you choose to show the power of God?

© Lauros - Giraudon / A.D.A.G.P /
Cathedral of Metz (France)

What Moses Discovered

Dromedary in the desert in Yemen

History

Moses* was born at the time when the children of Israel were in slavery and Hebrew baby boys were being killed. Moses' mother hid him in a basket by the river bank. He was found by the Pharaoh's daughter and brought up in the Egyptian palace.

When Moses grew up, he saw just how badly the Hebrew people were being treated. One day he attacked an Egyptian guard who had been beating a Hebrew slave. The Egyptian died, and Moses had to escape into the desert. There he had time to reflect in the silence of the desert. The thought of the Hebrew people being mistreated haunted him. Moses realized that God was calling him to free his people. It was like a bolt of lightning for him, like a raging fire.

How the Scriptures Tell the Story of Moses

Moses was by himself in the desert. There was no one else there when he realized that God was calling him. When God called to Moses from the burning bush (Exodus 3), he told him that the cruelty of the Egyptians did not go unnoticed. God was ready to deliver his people from bondage.

In the early books of the Bible, we can see that God often told Moses to write something down. This is one way we know that these stories really did happen, and that God has made sure that the events were recorded so his people would never forget.

Worker in Alexandria, Egypt

* Moses
Moses' name can mean "pulled from the water." It reflects the story of how Moses was rescued from the river by Pharaoh's daughter. (Exodus 2.5-10)

Yahweh
This is the personal name of the God of the Hebrews. It has several meanings. It can mean "the one who is always there for his people" or "the one who cannot fully be known" or even "the one who frees his people."

Covenant
The Bible often talks about the Covenant that God has with men and women. Because Abraham was asleep when God initiated the covenant with the Jewish people, it is called an "unconditional" covenant. This means that it will never be broken.

Bible

Go and Set My People Free!

Exodus 3.1-10 (excerpts)

One day, Moses was taking care of the sheep and goats of his father-in-law Jethro, the priest of Midian, and Moses decided to lead them across the desert to Sinai, the holy mountain. There an angel of the LORD appeared to him from a burning bush. Moses saw that the bush was on fire, but it was not burning up. "This is strange!" he said to himself. "I'll go over and see why the bush isn't burning up."

When the LORD saw Moses coming near the bush, he called him by name, and Moses answered, "Here I am."

God replied, "Don't come any closer. Take off your sandals – the ground where you are standing is holy. I am the God who was worshiped by your ancestors Abraham, Isaac, and Jacob."

Moses was afraid to look at God and so he hid his face.
The LORD said:

I have seen how my people are suffering as slaves in Egypt, and I have heard them beg for my help because of the way they are being mistreated. I feel sorry for them, and I have come down to rescue them from the Egyptians.

I will bring my people out of Egypt into a country where there is good land, rich with milk and honey…

Now go to the king! I am sending you to lead my people out of his country.

Jethro

Moses, wanted by the Egyptian police, took refuge in the desert. He was taken into Jethro's family and he married Jethro's daughter.

A Flame

No one can actually show what God looks like. So we use images and symbols. The Bible often uses fire when it wants to talk about the presence, the greatness, the beauty, and the mystery of God.

Holy Ground

Moses has to take off his sandals to show respect for a holy place. Today, in certain places of prayer, you still have to take off your shoes before going in.

Today

God's Name

Becoming More Aware

How can we ignore the injustice that stops many people from living like normal human beings? How can we stand by while so many wrongs go unpunished? We really need to become aware of situations that urgently need changing.

Call

Some men and women say to themselves, "Oppression and slavery are intolerable. They are crimes against humanity." When they become aware of this, it feels like an urgent call from God. They know they must get involved and fight against everything that is disrespectful of human beings and destroys their freedom.

God Gets Involved

Where can we look for God? In the Bible! In this collection of 66 books, God has given us his revealed word. This means that many things we cannot know (for instance, details about the creation of the world), God has provided for us in written form. So, too, did he make sure that the things that happened to his people in Egypt were written down so that future generations could understand how much he loved and watched over them.

God's Name

God's name is mysterious. God is a parent who looks after humans with the same love a parent has for a child. God became a human being in Jesus Christ the Son, so that he could share our human existence. God is the Holy Spirit who inspires people to create a friendly world where people live together like children loved by God.

Mission

God has entrusted each one of us with a mission to seek freedom for us and for others. Each one of us has been called to share the mission of Jesus. This call means working to stop evil from overcoming people. Faith means answering God's call and giving ourselves wholeheartedly to this mission of freedom.

Danger

You take a risk
when you oppose the hatred
that sets people
one against the other.

You take a risk
when you stand up for those
who are being mocked,
or welcome refugees.

You take a risk
when you work for human rights,
for fair shares for all
and a place for everyone,
especially the homeless and poor.

If you try to do this
you will risk being mocked,
misunderstood and rejected.
Yet it's the only way
for a human being
to truly live as a child of God.

CHAPTER 3

Set Free

Mozambic Bible
Moses closes the Red Sea on the Egyptians
tenth century, Spain

It looks as if the artist enjoyed painting the sea swallowing up the Egyptians. Look at the fish flying in all directions!

© Giraudon - Church of St. Isidore, Leon, Spain

Journey Out of Egypt

History

Rameses II in his war chariot
© Egyptian Museum, Cairo

When Moses was in the desert, he realized that God was calling him to free his people. So he went back to Egypt and, along with his brother Aaron, asked Pharaoh to let the children of Israel leave. But it was no use, because Pharaoh refused. At the same time, Moses explained to the people that it would be better for them to leave Egypt. And one spring* day the children of Israel set off. How did they manage to leave? God struck Egypt with unexpected disasters and made it possible for the Israelites to leave. Moses led the people — men, women, children, along with their flocks of animals — into the desert, to the Red Sea. A group of Pharaoh's soldiers set out to find and bring them back and they soon caught up to them at the edge of the sea. When the Egyptian army tried to cross through the dry path God had made in the sea, the water came crashing down and they drowned! The children of Israel saw the whole thing. For Moses and his people it was obvious: "The Lord threw the horses and their riders into the sea."**

Egyptian shepherd leading his flock

Exodus Celebrated

Israel was never to forget this event. Over the centuries, the story was read to large gatherings of Jews and they would remember what God had done for them, and they would rejoice and praise his name. They remembered that it was Yahweh who led his people by a column of fire, that Moses opened and closed the waters with a gesture of his hand, and that the whole of Pharaoh's army was engulfed in the waves. These stories are celebrations of how Yahweh miraculously freed the people.

* Spring
The journey out of Egypt took place in springtime, the season of the year when shepherds used to celebrate taking their flocks to pasture.

** The Sea Crossing
No one is exactly sure where the Israelites crossed the Red Sea, to escape Pharaoh's army, but archaeologists continue to look for evidence of this miraculous event from Israel's amazing past.

Bible

Victory Song
Exodus 14.5 – 5.20 (extracts)

When the king of Egypt heard that the Israelites had finally left, he and his officials changed their minds and said, "Look what we have done! We let them get away, and they will no longer be our slaves."

The king got his war chariot and army ready. He commanded his officers in charge of his six hundred best chariots and all his other chariots to start after the Israelites…

When the Israelites saw the king coming with his army, they were frightened and begged the LORD for help. They also complained to Moses, "Wasn't there enough room in Egypt to bury us? Is that why you brought us out here to die in the desert?…

But Moses answered, "Don't be afraid! Be brave, and you will see the LORD save you today… The LORD will fight for you, and you won't have to do a thing."…

The LORD drowned them in the sea…

On that day, when the Israelites saw the bodies of the Egyptians washed up on the shore, they knew that the LORD had saved them. Because of the mighty power he had used against the Egyptians, the Israelites worshiped him and trusted him and his servant Moses.

Moses and the Israelites sang this song in praise of the LORD:
> Sing praises to the LORD
>   for his great victory!
> He has thrown the horses and their riders
>   into the sea.

Miriam the sister of Aaron was a prophet. So she took her tambourine and led the other women out to play their tambourines and to dance.

Let Israel Go

According to the Bible account, several misfortunes (the plagues of Egypt) struck the country and forced the Pharaoh to let the children of Israel go.

Bringing Us Out

People call the Israelite's escape from Egypt the "Exodus." This comes from a Greek word meaning "the way out." It's also the title of the second book of the Bible, the book of Exodus.

On that Day

There are no Egyptian writings about Israel's exodus. The Egyptians were not interested in it. For the Israelites, on the other hand, the successful journey out of Egypt was an event of great importance. It was like the birth of their nation.

Today

Liberation

Standing Firm

When we are really distressed and our oppressors seem to be too powerful, it's difficult not to lose heart. God calls us not to give in to despair but to stand firm and hold our ground. Slowly but surely, God helps us to overturn things that oppress us.

God Saves

God never allows any of his children to remain prisoners of those who seek to dominate people and to cause misery. He loosens the grip of the chains of evil and frees people. He saves them! Jesus came among us to save us from the penalty for sin, which is eternal separation from God.

Exodus

The journey out of Egypt – the Exodus – has become a symbol. It symbolizes captive people being set free. The Exodus is also a symbol that we feel inside us: God calling us all, with his help, to break free from the grip of sin.

Passover and Easter

Every year Jewish people celebrate Passover, the anniversary of the journey out of Egypt, the passing from slavery to freedom. Every year Christians celebrate Passover, the passing from death to life in the Christian Easter. The risen Jesus frees people from the slavery of death.

Praise

People who trust in God give thanks because they believe that in a mysterious way, God is at their side when they are being set free. Christians give thanks for Jesus, the Son of God.

Amazing God

How amazing God is!

God stands alongside
the humble,
the persecuted,
those who are mocked
and laughed at.

How great God is!
God's almighty power
is at the service of the poor:
restoring the dignity of those
who are bowed down,
crushed by oppressors
and despised by others.

Yesterday, today
and for all the days to come
God sings a song of freedom
in the hearts of the oppressed.
To those who have been
denied justice,
God gives power
for freedom and liberty.

How amazing God is!

CHAPTER 4
The Ten Commandments

Jacopo di Paolo
(fourteenth-fifteenth century)
Moses Presenting the Tablets of the Law to the People
Bologna school, Fresco

The painting tells the story of the gift of the Law.
Can you see Moses in two places in the picture?
What is he doing?

© Alinari-Giraudon / National Gallery of Painting, Bologna (Italy)

Learning To Live Together

History

Mount Sinai in present-day Egypt

Israel left Egypt. The slaves are now free, but the rough life in the desert is about to begin. People have to learn how to travel day after day in search of water, to be satisfied with a basic diet, to live together in tents and take to the road together. They have to agree to laws that everyone will obey. Little by little, the band of former slaves becomes an organized people. Their leader is Moses and their God is Yahweh. One day they make an extraordinary discovery. Until now they had been living on the plain.* Now they come to the foot of an impressive mountain – Sinai. They experience a thunderstorm on the mountain. It's a marvelous, but terrifying experience, because they understood the thunderstorm to be a sign of God's presence among them. Following that theophany (a sign of God's presence) God enters into a covenant with the people, so that they become the people of God.

A man sifting grain in Egypt

Moses the Great Lawgiver**

There are very many laws in the Bible. Some date from the time of Moses. Others were written later. These laws govern life in a society made up of shepherds and farmers. They tell people how to live in peace with one another and with God. The people of Israel understood these laws as coming directly from God. For Israel, obeying the laws (or the Law) meant keeping the covenant with God. The core of these laws can be summarized in the collection we call the "Ten Commandments."

* On the plain
Until this time the children of Israel had lived in the Nile Delta, a rich, fertile region in Egypt built up from soil deposited from the river. The plain was a large, level, treeless area.

** The lawgiver
A legislator, or lawgiver, is a person who makes the law. In the Bible, Moses is considered as the one responsible for all the laws.

Bible

Moses Receives the Law

Exodus 19.1 – 20.17 (extracts)

Two months after leaving Egypt, they arrived at the desert near Mount Sinai, where they set up camp at the foot of the mountain…

On the morning of the third day there was thunder and lightning… a loud trumpet blast was heard, and everyone in camp trembled with fear…

Mount Sinai was covered with smoke because the LORD had come down in a flaming fire. Smoke poured out of the mountain just like a furnace, and the whole mountain shook. The trumpet blew louder and louder. Moses spoke, and God answered him with thunder…

God said to the people of Israel:

I am the LORD your God, the one who brought you out of Egypt.

Do not worship any god except me.

Do not misuse my name.

Remember that the Sabbath Day belongs to me.

Respect your father and your mother.

Do not murder.

Be faithful in marriage.

Do not steal.

Do not tell lies about others.

Do not want anything that belongs to someone else.

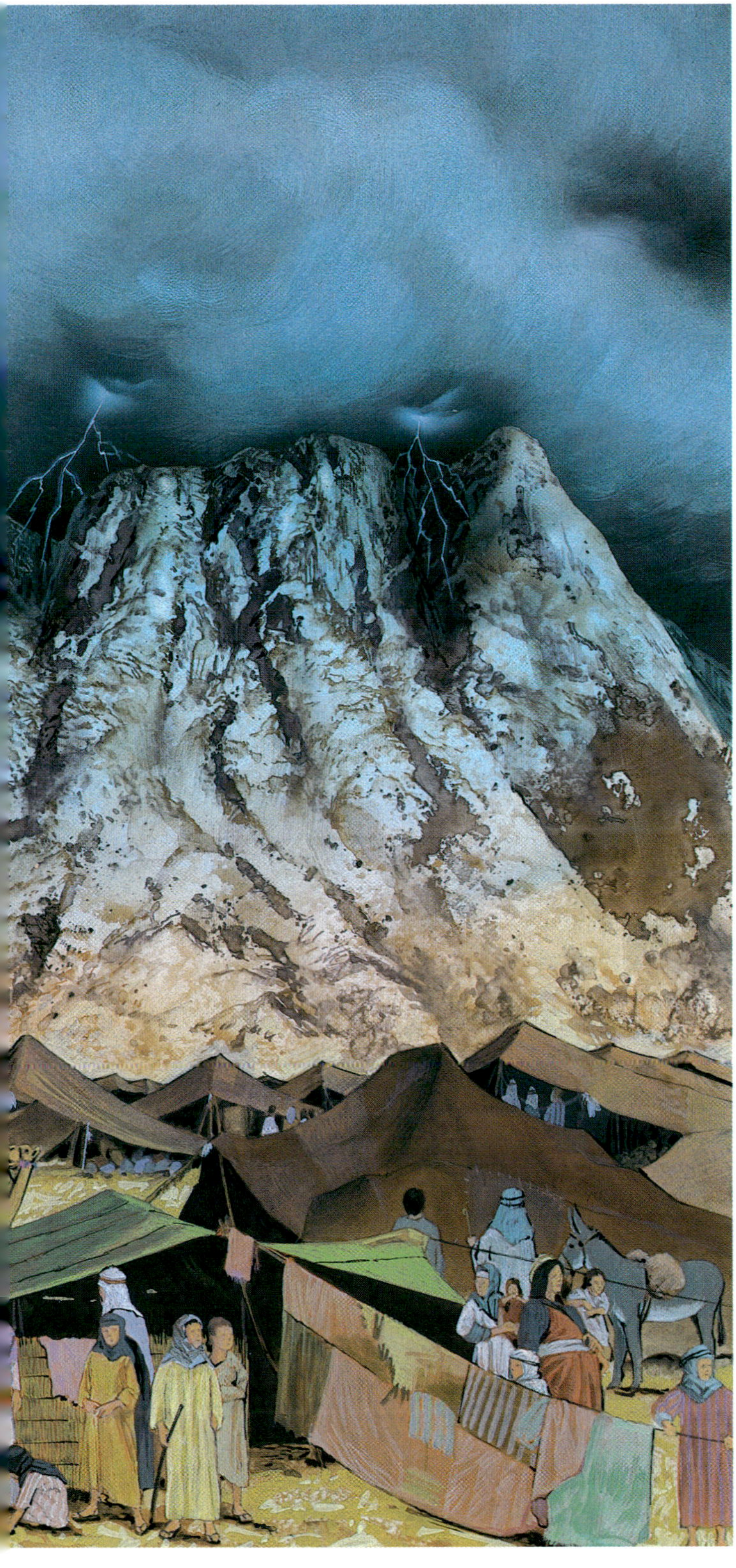

Thunder

The people were terrified when they heard thunder on the mountain; they understood that God is all-powerful. They were very reverent, and decided that they were not worthy to be in God's presence.

His Words

According to other passages of the Bible, these words were carved on two stone tablets, called the tablets of the Law.

The Sabbath

The Sabbath (our Saturday) is a day of rest that the people of the Bible dedicate to God, because he commands us to remember that he rested after creating the heavens and the earth.

Today

Getting Involved

Marching
Being set free is such a joyful event! It can happen in a day, but living a life of freedom, with all its daily problems, is a bit harder to do. It's like going on a journey. You have to decide for yourself which road to take, what useless baggage to get rid of, and how to be happy with just the essentials.

Living Together
How do people on such a long journey live together and respect each other? Who should decide who's right and who's wrong? We have to be clear about everyone's role so that we can organize our lives and live in peace. If everyone makes his or her own decisions without bothering about others, can there be order or progress?

Laws
It's impossible to make any progress along the road if we don't all freely agree to obey certain laws. Our Code of Law is what allows us to live happily and to respect each other.

Ten Commandments
The Ten Commandments come from God. They are laws. The first three are about our duties toward God. The other seven are about our duties toward our neighbors. They sum up what we have to do to love God and our neighbors.

Covenant
God made a covenant with the Jewish people. The covenant stated that they would inherit the Land of Canaan, and much more territory, and that it would be an everlasting possession for the descendants of Isaac, Abraham's son. In fact, God changed the name of Isaac's son, Jacob, to Israel.

Freedom!

Ten words of freedom,
ten ways to walk free,
the Ten Commandments
are God's gift to me.

He gives them to all
to obey through the year,
they're words God speaks
for all hearts to hear.

Light for the darkness
to drive evil away,
a pattern for life
to guide us each day.

Beacons to lead us
and draw us to God,
finding a path
that so many have walked.

Ten words to shape us
so all will see:
We are God's people
loving and free.

CHAPTER 5
Toward the Promised Land

Lord of the Manna
(fifteenth century)
Harvest of the Manna
Netherlands, painting on wood

The artist wants to show that manna is a gift from God. How does he do this?

© Giraudon - Museum of Chartreuse, Douai (France)

The Road Continues

H i s t o r y

Ingeburg Psalter, Denmark
Worshiping the golden calf. About 1210
© Giraudon - Condé Museum, Chantilly (France)

After their stop at Sinai, the people continued on their journey across the desert to Canaan, the Promised Land. It was a long way, the road was hard and not everyone agreed that they should go on. Some people missed the rich food they used to eat in Egypt. Others criticized Moses and wanted another leader. People began to doubt Yahweh. At one time, the people made themselves a golden calf that they worshiped as if it were their god. Some people wanted to get straight to the Promised Land, but others wanted to settle at an oasis in Kadesh.* It wasn't always easy for Moses. When he got discouraged he turned to Yahweh. However, he stayed on the road with his people until they reached Mount Nebo, opposite Jericho. From there he could see the Promised Land. But he was not to enter it.

Carving of stalks of wheat from Luxor, Egypt

Remembering This Long Journey

The Bible people often thought about that long journey in the desert. It was a little like everyone's life. God helped people along that road by sending them an extraordinary food, manna** and quails. He had helped them to find water in a surprising way. He had rescued them from their enemies who were attacking them. Among the good memories were some of terrible times. The people were "stiff necked." They moaned all the time about Moses and God. That's why the Bible writers said that they stayed forty years in the desert. That was the length of time it took for a new generation to grow up, who had learned to trust God. It was that new generation who would enter the Promised Land as God's people.

* Kadesh
The oasis of Kadesh, in the south of Canaan, was one of the great stopping places on the journey through the desert. It was when they left there that the Israelites set off to explore the Promised Land.

** Manna
The word means "what's this?" after the reaction of the Israelites when they found it in the desert. Manna was like a white flake and the miraculous food was picked up every day by the Israelites.

Bible

The Death of Moses
Deuteronomy 34.1-10 (extracts)

Sometime later, Moses left the lowlands of Moab. He went up Mount Pisgah to the peak of Mount Nebo, which is across the Jordan River from Jericho. The LORD showed him all the land…

The LORD said, "Moses, this is the land I was talking about when I solemnly promised Abraham, Isaac, and Jacob that I would give land to their descendants. I have let you see it, but you will not cross the Jordan and go in."

And so, Moses the LORD's servant died there in Moab, just as the LORD had said. The LORD buried him in a valley near the town of Beth-Peor, but even today no one knows exactly where. Moses was a hundred twenty years old when he died, yet his eyesight was still good, and his body was strong.

The people of Israel stayed in the lowlands of Moab, where they mourned and grieved thirty days for Moses…

There has never again been a prophet in Israel like Moses. The LORD spoke face to face with him.

The Whole Land

This refers to the Promised Land. Today it is Israel.

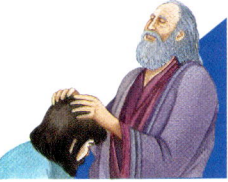

Thirty Days

After these thirty days, Joshua, whom Moses had chosen, replaced him as leader of the people. He was the one who would lead Israel into the Promised Land.

Face to Face

The Israelites thought it was impossible to see God without dying. They thought that they had to turn their face away from God. Moses was an exception.

Today

Faithfulness

Life's Road
Some days we travel life's road with great courage, but on other days we feel weak and would like to stop. We can only make progress along this road if we keep trying and don't give up when obstacles come along. That's the price of getting to our destination.

Desert
The scenery on the road of life is always changing. The way may be filled with laughter, fear, love, distress, loneliness or happiness. Sometimes the road passes through the desert. On those days, everything seems dry, unsuccessful and miserable. "Deserts" test the courage of everyone on the journey.

Doubts
When they got into difficulty in the desert, some people began to doubt: "Why should we put so much effort into keeping the Ten Commandments? Is it worth all this trouble to believe in God? Why should we continue trusting God when everything keeps going wrong?"

Idols
Some people complained to God, "You're not bothered about us !" They began to love and trust "idols." They began to prefer gold, glory and selfish pleasures. They made these their "gods" to serve and honor.

Stiff Neck
Some translations say the Israelites were self willed or stiff necked. People find it hard to "bend" themselves to obey the Ten Commandments. Their hearts and spirits become stiff. They forget that being faithful to God's commandments and the Covenant is nothing more than a sign of our love for God.

The Promised Land

isn't only a land
with trees, fields and houses.
It's the goal
that those who trust in God
are all aiming for.
We'll reach that goal one day,
at the end of time,
when God's children
will pass through death
and live in his presence,
beautiful and free.

The road to the Promised Land
has been marked out clearly
by Jesus Christ himself:
loving God and our neighbor;
living in truth;
feeding the hungry;
rescuing the poor;
showing mercy;
giving a place
to those who have been rejected;
building a world of justice;
putting our trust in the Father
who is in heaven;
acting according to the Son's word;
opening ourselves
to the power of the Spirit!
It's easy to check
whether or not
we're on our way to
the Promised Land!

INSIGHTS

Human Rights

The story of Moses is about people being set free. The Ten Commandments, given through Moses, set the guidelines for life as a free people. They are like a first draft of human rights.

Take a look at the commandments on page 22, and see whether you can find the following: right to a reputation, right of respect owed to parents, right to rest, right to a faithful love, right to truth, right to property, and right to have your life respected.

Not always respected

But in our world today, there are still millions of slaves, men women, and children.

There are people in prison because they don't believe what their rulers want them to believe. There are millions of people who don't have enough food to keep them from being hungry; who never manage to learn how to read and write; who are denied a decent place to live; who lack care when they are sick; who are prevented from having a happy life. Human rights are far from being respected. Moses' story is not over yet.

Obeying God

John the apostle tells us in one of his letters that true love is obeying God and his commandments. Today, Jews and Gentiles are still called to this kind of obedience, which pleases God. People are not so different from the ancient Israelites; some follow God, but many do not.

A Lesson for Us

Even though it sometimes seems that God has stopped caring about us, or no longer hears us, in fact, he is paying very close attention to our circumstances.

It is important to remember that Moses' story is true, so that we have confidence that God saved the ancient Israelites in a spectacular way, and also is able and willing to save those who call on him in our own time.

The Bible tells us that nothing can separate a child of God from the love of God. That is his promise to us, now and for all time.

Titles already published:

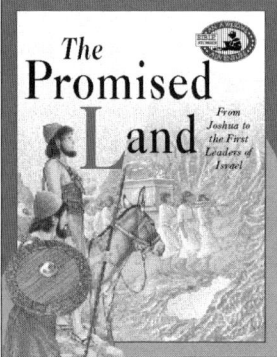

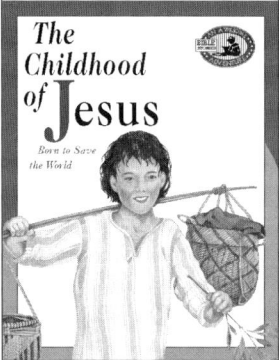

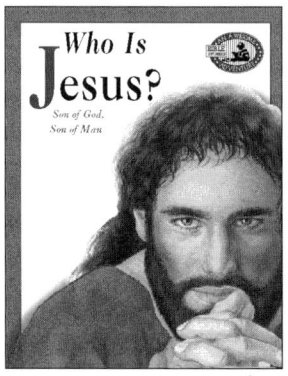

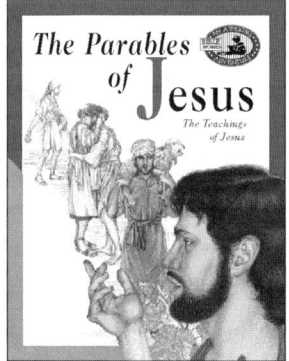

Forthcoming titles in the JUNIOR BIBLE Collection:

- The First Prophets
- Passion and Resurrection
- Exile and Return
- Isaiah, Micah, Jeremiah
- Jesus and the Outcasts
- Jesus in Jerusalem
- Acts
- Wisdom
- Psalms
- Women
- Revelation
- Letters

The Long Journey with Moses

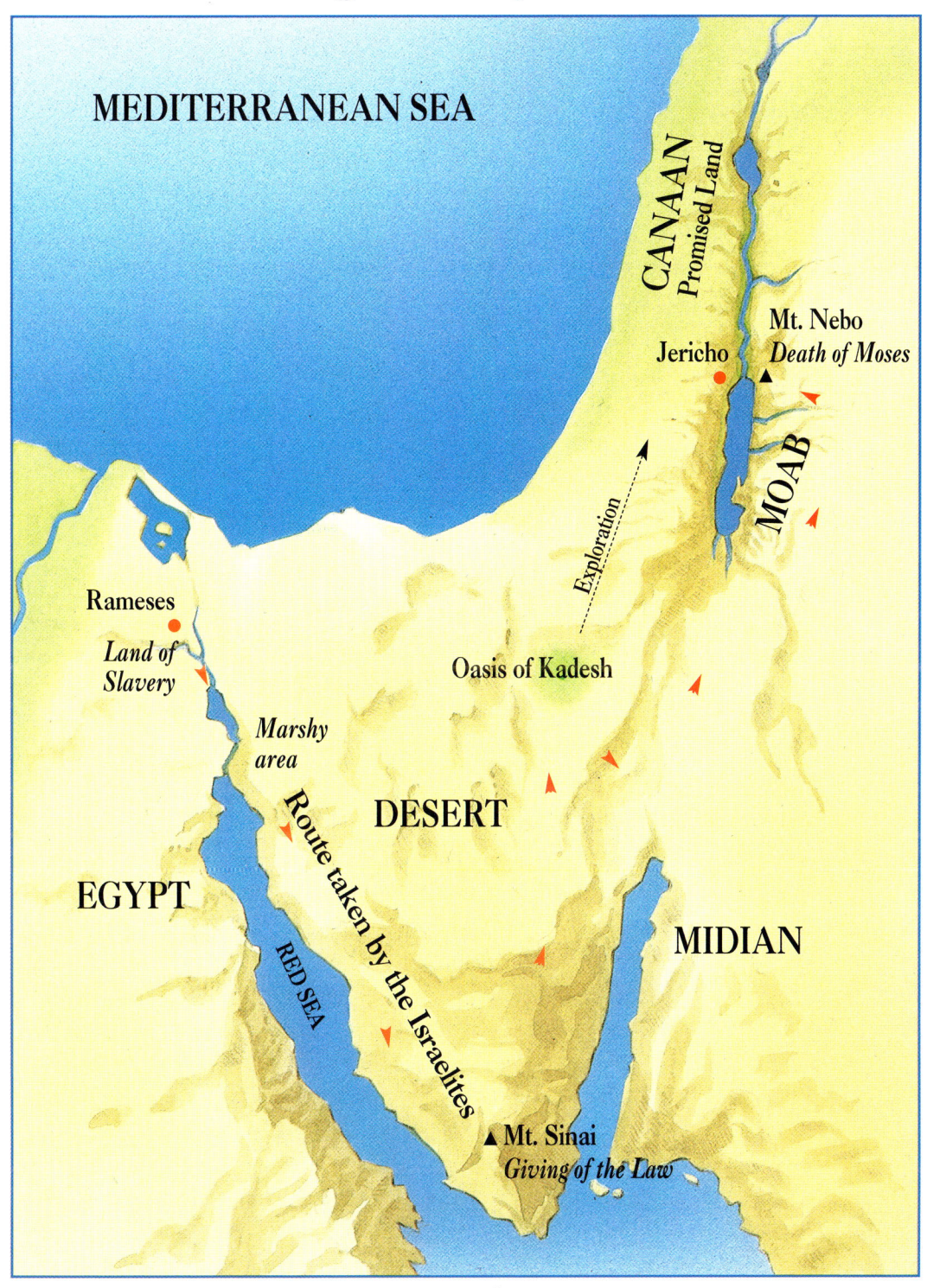

→ Route of the Israelites from slavery to the Promised Land

Moses

ORIGINAL TEXT BY
Liam KELLY, Anne WHITE,
Albert HARI, Charles SINGER

ENGLISH TEXT ADAPTED BY
the American Bible Society

PHOTOGRAPHY
Frantisek ZVARDON, Gabriel LOISON,
Patrice THÉBAULT

ILLUSTRATORS
Mariano VALSESIA, Betti FERRERO
MIA. Milan Illustrations Agency

LAYOUT
Bayle Graphic Studio

FIRST PRINTING: NOVEMBER 2000

Copyright © 2000 by Master Books
for the CBA U.S. edition.

All rights reserved. Printed in Italy. No part of this book may be used or reproduced in any manner whatsoever without written permission of the publisher except in the case of brief quotations in articles and reviews.

For information write: Master Books, P.O. Box 727, Green Forest, AR 72638.

ISBN: 0-89051-325-2

© ÉDITIONS DU SIGNE 1997